High Technology and American Foreign Policy

Lawrence S. Eagleburger

LAWRENCE S. EAGLEBURGER is president of Kissinger Associates, Inc., which he joined in 1984 after serving for twenty-seven years in various positions at the Department of State. From 1982 to 1984 he was under secretary of state for political affairs, the third highest position in the department. Previously he served as assistant secretary of state for European affairs, ambassador to Yugoslavia, deputy under secretary of state for management, executive assistant to Secretary of State Kissinger, deputy assistant secretary of defense, and deputy assistant to the president for national security affairs. Mr. Eagleburger has received the Distinguished Civilian Service Medal from the Department of Defense, the President's Award for Distinguished Federal Civilian Service, and the Department of State Distinguished Honor Award. He is a member of the board of directors of the ITT Corporation, Sedco, and Ljubljanska Banka.

ISBN 0-8447-1375-9

Printed in the United States of America

American Enterprise Institute for Public Policy Research
1150 Seventeenth Street, N.W., Washington, D.C. 20036

Introduction

William J. Baroody
President
American Enterprise Institute

G. Warren Nutter was one of the great conservative intellectuals of his time. He was a scholar and statesman who understood better than most the importance of ideas in the development of public policy. He worked closely with my father, the late William J. Baroody, Sr., to foster new ideas and to create an environment in which the American Enterprise Institute and other public policy research organizations are able to flourish.

Warren taught for many years at the University of Virginia and was chairman of its economics department in the late 1960s. He took leave from 1969 to 1973 to serve as assistant secretary of defense for international security affairs. He was awarded the Defense Department's Distinguished Public Service Medal for his service there. He was a specialist in several aspects of economics: the economics of defense, industrial organization, the Soviet economy, and general microeconomic theory.

I had the privilege of knowing Warren beginning when I was very young, when he would join my father and other scholars at our home for dinner and discussion. Many times in recent years I have looked at the turns public policy has taken and thought back to what Warren Nutter said about the role of government in free societies. He advocated a greater balance between the public and private sectors.

"The question at issue," he wrote, "is not whether Americans should believe in either individualism or collectivism. Neither is adequate to serve by itself as the philosophic foundation of a viable democratic republic. The underlying philosophy must be a mixture of both. But it is critically important which dominates."[1]

1. G. Warren Nutter, *Political Economy and Freedom: A Collection of Essays*, edited by Jane Couch Nutter (Indianapolis: Liberty Press, 1983), p. 57.

He believed individualism was essential to individual liberty, and his life and his teachings were testaments to this idea.

The American Enterprise Institute, together with thinking Americans everywhere, owes a lasting debt to Warren Nutter. His integrity and his scholarship serve as a guiding light to those who carry on his life's mission. We are proud to present these memorial lectures as a tribute to him and as a forum for the continued competition of ideas that he treasured. Today's speaker, Lawrence Sidney Eagleburger, is an outstanding American statesman who is also an old friend.

There are many of us working around Washington—both in government and in the private sector—who will be forever grateful for the guidance and leadership we received from the likes of Warren Nutter and Melvin Laird. Larry Eagleburger and I are clearly in that category.

Larry today joins a distinguished group of scholars and statesmen who have given the Nutter Lectures at AEI. The lecturers are selected in cooperation with the trustees of the Thomas Jefferson Foundation—which was founded by Warren Nutter and James Buchanan in 1957—and they fall generally into three categories: former academic colleagues of Professor Nutter, including S. Herbert Frankel, Milton Friedman, R.H. Coase, and George J. Stigler; former students of his, such as Paul Craig Roberts; and former government colleagues, such as Admiral Thomas H. Moorer, Yuan-li Wu, and our most recent lecturer, Roger E. Shields.

Larry worked with Warren Nutter at the Pentagon in the first Nixon administration. He had one of those long titles that make life at the Department of Defense so much fun: deputy assistant secretary of defense for policy plans and National Security Council affairs.

He worked with Warren on a wide range of issues, including the negotiations in Vienna for a mutual balanced force reduction. He went from there to become principal aide to Henry Kissinger at the White House, then at the State Department. As many of you know, the relationship between Larry Eagleburger and Henry Kissinger has been a long and fruitful one that continues to this day—Larry is president of Kissinger Associates, a "somewhat successful" consulting firm formed by the former secretary of state.

I was a special assistant to Mel Laird while Larry was the key aide to Henry Kissinger, and I must say we had some interesting exchanges in those days. You may be assured that the turf battles among the State Department, the Defense Department, and the National Security Council predate Cap Weinberger and George Shultz.

I never worried about Larry, however. He may have spent a career at the State Department—he served there twenty-seven years in all—but his heart was in Wisconsin, his and Mel Laird's home state. In fact, I believe his mother was very active in Mel's first congressional campaign.

Larry Eagleburger worked his way up in the State Department and became one of this nation's foremost experts on European affairs and one of its most influential foreign policy makers. He served as a distinguished ambassador to Yugoslavia, chief of the political mission to NATO, assistant secretary of state for European affairs, and under secretary of state for political affairs. In all these roles, he has been a vital force in keeping the Western Alliance strong and in protecting U.S. interests in that region and in other parts of the world.

I am pleased to introduce our tenth Nutter lecturer, Mr. Lawrence Eagleburger.

High Technology and American Foreign Policy

Lawrence S. Eagleburger

I first met Warren Nutter in 1971 when he was assistant secretary of defense for international security affairs, and I had been recalled from an overseas assignment to be interviewed for a job as one of his deputies. It was an interesting meeting. Although he never quite said so, I suspect that from Warren's point of view he had been asked to consider hiring a cookie-pushing, soft, wrong-thinking, vaguely leftist Foreign Service officer. His lack of enthusiasm for the exercise was readily apparent to the sensitive, perspicacious fellow I then was.

From my perspective, I had been invited, like Daniel, into the lion's den. ISA had never been popular in the State Department for reasons not hard to fathom. For the Foreign Service it is a self-evident proposition that amateurs should never be permitted near the intricacies of foreign affairs. Yet, there were all those professors, politicians, and GS civilians substituting their judgments for those of the Foreign Service. Worse, they were in the Defense Department, which everyone knew was populated by pushy, hard-nosed, wrong-thinking, right-wing nuts.

The interview, somewhat akin to a meeting between a cobra and a mongoose, led soon thereafter—and somewhat to my surprise—to a job offer. I returned to Washington and ISA, and Warren immediately went on an extended vacation. I have no doubt that had my mother not been a long-time admirer and supporter of the then secretary of defense when he represented Wisconsin's Seventh Congressional District, I would never have been interviewed—much less employed—by the Defense Department.

From that less than auspicious beginning, I grew to have great affection, respect, and admiration for Warren. I rapidly came to appreciate his superb mind, which moved so quickly through problems that confounded the rest of us; I just as rapidly learned that here was a man who better than most understood the greatness of his country and the challenges, foreign and domestic, that threatened that greatness. Last but by no means least, I came to know a warm and decent human being who proved to be a kind teacher and a good friend.

It was therefore with real pleasure that I accepted the invitation to speak today in memory of, and in honor of, a man who has been rightly described by William Baroody, Jr., as "one of the great conservative intellectuals of his time."

I have for some time been fascinated by the potential impact on our foreign policy of the revolution in technology we now see gaining momentum around us. Last year, shortly before I left the State Department, I suggested in a speech that not only was America's attention turning away from Europe toward the Pacific Basin, but that the worrisome evidence that our European friends and partners were falling behind in the high-technology race could further strain the transatlantic relationship in the years ahead. The reaction to that speech, particularly in Europe, was less than laudatory. *Le Monde,* in questioning my wisdom and paternity, remarked that I did not even have the excuse of being from California.

In the course of the past year, since I left government and, as a consequence, am permitted to think, I have become ever more convinced that, despite *Le Monde,* the changes taking place, and yet to occur, in high technology—particularly changes in information systems technology—will have profound domestic and international consequences. The foreign policy ramifications of the explosion of high technology in information systems are what I propose to examine with you today. Let me begin by stating the three propositions that form the outline of my approach.

- First, we are entering an era of revolutionary change occasioned by technological breakthroughs in the way we develop, store, process, transfer, and use information.
- Second, the United States will be uniquely able to sustain and exploit this "revolution."
- Third, as the United States moves more deeply into what future historians may well describe as another Industrial Revolution, we will find ourselves facing an international environment that is inevitably more complex—but an environment made even more complex be-

cause we are coping so much better than others with the challenges of a new era. Our very success could, instead of enhancing international stability and security, adversely affect our relations with friends and allies, adversaries, and the developing world alike.

If my own research and conversations with businessmen and academics are any indication, there is substantial consensus that the developed world, with the United States and Japan in the lead, will undergo, between now and the end of the century, revolutionary changes in the efficiency with which we store, process, transfer, and use information. There is, as well, general acceptance of the proposition that this "revolution" will profoundly affect our social and economic environment, creating opportunities that are today unimaginable.

Here are some relevant facts and predictions:

- The manufacture of information technology today produces yearly revenues for U.S. companies of some $110 billion, which is some 3.3 percent of our gross national product, and about equal to the yearly activity of the automobile industry. By 1994 the information industry's yearly revenues will be $330 billion, or 6 percent of U.S. GNP.
- Before 1990, information technology will be the world's largest manufacturing industry.
- Given expected improvements in existing technology, plus predictable developments in new technology, computers will provide at least 100 times more power within ten years, at costs roughly comparable to those of today. An improvement of 1,000 times over today's computers cannot be more than two decades away.
- There are now more than 6 million computers in the United States, and some estimate that one-half of all U.S. households will have a computer-based system by 1990.

These are but a few examples of what is already under way around us. Microprocessor chips the size of a fingernail can already be combined in machines the size of a dining room table that would hold all of the information contained in the Library of Congress. Optical disks the size of a long-playing record are now being developed that will be capable of storing on one disk all the information now contained in all the world's telephone books.

I do not pretend to know what our lives will be like as we enter the twenty-first century, but that they will be substantially different seems inevitable. No one can easily predict how individual countries will react to, or take advantage of, the information revolution. Nevertheless, the competition for leadership in the development and exploitation of information systems technology will be intense. What can we say about the future of this competition? Which nations are likely to be most successful? Which less so?

The United States, I believe, enjoys such substantial advantages that it would take monumental government ineptitude and an industrial mind set akin to that of the U.S. automobile industry of the 1960s and 1970s to keep us from leading the way into this new era. Japan, almost certainly, will be close behind; Western Europe is much more uncertain; and the Soviet Union is likely to be condemned to second-class status in the absence of fundamental systemic changes. I come to these conclusions because of three factors that will be critical in determining how the protagonists will perform: the size of the market, the society's orientation toward "engineering," and the existence of an entrepreneurial culture.

Market Size

Whatever else one can say about the development of the new information technology, it is brutally obvious that it will be expensive. High-technology research costs, plus the costs of translating those research findings into products for sale, tax many of our largest companies and have already driven many others—foreign and domestic—out of business. Those costs, as competition becomes more fierce, will grow rapidly. A major factor in the ability to remain in the game will thus be the size of the market available to support the industry.

The American market is now, and is likely to continue to be for some time, the largest single consumer of computer hardware and software and other information systems products. It is, as well, still the freest market, as names such as Fujitsu, Toshiba, and Mitsubishi demonstrate. U.S. firms, through a series of interlocking agreements with Japanese and European firms, are also moving to strengthen their access to foreign markets and to cooperative R & D schemes. IBM, for example, has entered into one agreement that includes relationships with twelve semiconductor makers, two computer manufacturers, and two telecommunications companies, all of which involve five countries.

Even at this relatively early stage we see a whole range of information-related industrial giants working hard to ensure access to as wide a market as possible. Yet there are countertrends as well. Japan remains unprepared to permit meaningful access to its domestic information market, as it does with so many other industries. I am told, however, that such firms as IBM have been able to beat the Japanese on their home ground more than once and remain confident they can continue to do so, particularly in software.

The Western European market—or more aptly, the various national markets in Western Europe—remain open to foreign firms, particularly if the foreign companies have working relationships with companies located within the various European countries. Yet evidence of growing European concern over the state of its information industry could engender protectionist pressures. The Esprit program of the European Economic Community (EEC), an effort to develop a Common Market information technology, envisages EEC Commission, member government, and private industry cooperation aimed at overtaking the U.S. and Japanese lead in information systems in ten years. Imaginative as this program may prove to be, it is avowedly aimed at taking the European market away from U.S. and Japanese firms, though even here one must wonder if it can be truly successful with so many U.S. companies already present in Europe through subsidiaries or cooperative agreements of one kind or another.

In sum, then, market size is critical—and increasingly so—to the ability of information technology industries to recoup their R & D costs. Both the United States and Japan have access to large markets—the United States to its own and the fragmented European market, the Japanese to those markets and its own as well. Whether that will continue to be the case for the Japanese remains to be seen. They seem well on their way to awakening the sleeping giant for the second time in this century; should the United States move to shut out or restrict severely Japanese computer or electronics exports, Japan's market would shrink overnight, with serious consequences to Japanese competitive abilities.

Western Europe's problem is of a different character; no common Western European market exists for the products of its various high-technology industries. As *The Economist* (London) for November 24–30, 1984, said in a superb article on Europe's technology gap:

> Young, innovative European firms labour under crippling burdens that their American and Japanese counterparts do not have. One—the uncommon market—is well known, though the extent of the damage it does is not. Testing and

> certification requirements, differing standards, border delays and restraints on trade in services all take their toll on trade between EEC countries. These obstacles add as much as 20% to the cost of goods in intracommunity trade. . . . And the effects of Europe's market fragmentation are getting worse all the time: as development costs rise and product lives contract, it becomes even harder to recoup investment in a single national market.

In 1983 the EEC accounted for 30 percent of the world market for information technology. Yet the community was able to capture only some 10 percent of that world market; its share of the European market was only 30 percent. These facts seem to prove fairly conclusively that Western European technology—or at least its practical application—is not up to American or Japanese standards. The Esprit program previously referred to may do something to improve this situation, but we are nonetheless left to wonder how much can really be accomplished until and unless the Common Market countries get back to the business of building Europe. Arguing over milk quotas, corn gluten, or even budgets may keep bureaucrats and politicians off the streets, but it is unproductive work compared with the truly crucial task of building a market sufficient to support the R & D costs that must form the base of a healthy and competitive information industry in the last decade and a half of the century.

Orientation toward Engineering

Harder to define, but equally critical to exploiting successfully the new information technologies, is the degree to which a society is oriented toward engineering in its broadest sense—a society that is comfortable with new technologies and knows how to use them. American GIs during World War II were unique among combatants in their familiarity with things mechanical. When the engine on the truck gave up, someone was inevitably able to fix it because he had grown up tinkering with the family car or tractor.

America is now in the process of building a nation that is comfortable with the computer—comfortable with our movement toward an information culture. My eleven-year-old son already speaks a language full of "modems," "mouse," "RAMs," etc.—a language I only pretend to understand. His generation certainly will be as comfortable with, and as dependent upon, the computer and its ancillary equipment as we are the automobile or the telephone. These are the people who will transform the information revolution from the new and mysterious to the commonplace and essential.

The United States is perhaps the world's only truly revolutionary society. We are a people who are comfortable with change; we often seek change for its own sake. New inventions intrigue us; new gimmicks bring us to the stores in droves. We are also a people who will not rest until we have found new uses for the devices our technology creates. So the information revolution in this country will fall on fertile ground—not just as something that scientists, businessmen, bureaucrats, and educators can use, but as something that the most average among us will sooner or later find to be an intimate part of everyday life.

As in so many things, Japan is hard to classify in this respect. Certainly it is a nation of great technological imagination and ingenuity, a nation that must, therefore, be classified as an "engineering-oriented" society. Yet, it is as well a nation profoundly conservative in its traditions and culture, with a homogenous population that has known little of the daily turmoil and change that are the everyday fare of an America of varying religions, racial makeup, and global responsibilities.

It may be that Japan will be able to contend with the revolutionary impact of the information explosion on its society and culture. Given the record, one would have to argue so. Nevertheless, the strains on the system may prove to be intense. In any event, I suspect that the United States will be better able to cope with the inevitable changes than will Japan.

At first blush most Western European nations appear to be societies comfortable with technological change. Further examination leads to a more qualified view. Try as I have to find authorities in any of the current literature who would argue that Europeans—or some European nations—are at the forefront of technological development over a broad spectrum, I could find none. Certain industries in certain countries do well. The general consensus remains, however, that Europe is falling further behind in the high-technology race. Let me quote again from the same *Economist* article:

> Few doubt that Europe is in real trouble. There are two reasons, one specific, the other much broader. The specific worry is Europe's poor performance in the information industries. . . . The general worry is Europe's inability to inno-

vate: its sluggishness in creating the new businesses, high-tech and low, which alone can generate growth and jobs.

There are many reasons for this phenomenon, not least of which is the "little Europe" thinking that has led to the "uncommon market" already discussed. Another, I believe, is that throughout the postwar years Europeans have opted for security over innovation. There has been a steady trend in every important Western European country toward the kinds of social legislation that inevitably make industry less able to adjust to changing times and market demands. I intend no social commentary here: certainly one could argue—though I would not—that European labor legislation, for example, is more humane than ours. Even if that were true, however, a cost has been exacted, not only in the dollars and cents terms that economists can quantify but in psychological terms as well. To generalize excessively to make my point, Europe has chosen the stability of predictability, and in the process lost the taste for change and challenge that was probably never as strong as it was and is in the United States.

The Entrepreneurial Culture

Of the three factors critical to the development of the new information society, the importance of an entrepreneurial culture should require the least discussion. The willingness—both personal and corporate—to take a chance is highly developed in the United States. And despite the concerns voiced by many that we are losing our entrepreneurial spirit, the facts seem to prove otherwise:

- In 1983 approximately 600,000 new corporations were established in the United States.
- Over 7 million *net* new jobs have been generated in the United States over the past two years, with much of this increase coming from companies with fewer than 200 workers.

Silicon Valley has rightly become famous as the outward manifestation of what risk taking in the field of information systems high technology can produce—the failures as well as the successes. It is a uniquely American institution, based on the concept of risk, but reinforced by other highly developed support mechanisms.

Our venture capital system, for example, provides an efficient means of assisting small firms to get their start. In 1983, $2.8 billion was committed to start-ups in the United States. Our tax system, at least until now, has tended to favor risk takers; our share option system rewards risk takers handsomely. In short, America's entrepreneurial spirit remains strong, and is supported by institutions, public and private, that raise the risk taker's odds of success appreciably.

It is certain that as the information revolution proceeds over the next decades many more companies seeking to be a part of that process will fail than will succeed. If history is any precedent, however, the successes will be noteworthy, with the probability that the end of the century will see new industrial giants that today can only be imagined. What is hard to see is how the information revolution could take place without these risk takers. The computer industry could not have advanced as it has were it not for the intense competition that developed to produce ever more efficient microchips and semiconductors. The same will remain true in the years ahead; the pace of change will be affected by the development of new industries finding new ways to use the new technologies, and thereby creating demand for newer technologies, newer applications of those technologies, and so on, ad infinitum.

Can Japan do as well? While the United States is a nation that prides itself on its individual entrepreneurs, Japan is a nation of collective risk takers. Japanese industry, often encouraged by government, finances and provides the personnel for new ventures. The system has certainly, thus far, proved successful and imaginative. But in an ever more complex environment one can at least be permitted to wonder whether this structured system can be as productive as the semichaotic but probably much more broadly based system we enjoy.

One must, again, be pessimistic about Western Europe. Individual entrepreneurs exist, to be sure. But the habit and concept of risk taking as we know it is by no means so deeply engrained in the European psyche. Nor are the institutions necessary to support risk takers particularly well developed. The *Economist* article mentioned previously notes, for example, that risk capital, except in Britain, is in short supply throughout Europe, with investment running at only some 10 to 20 percent of U.S. levels. The *International Herald Tribune* just yesterday carried an article on venture capital in Europe; while arguing that more effort is being made to support high-technology industries than in the past, it also admitted that the amount of risk capital available was minuscule when compared with the United States. Under such circumstances, one can but wonder if the question of whether there are any entrepreneurs in Europe is particularly relevant, since the means to finance them, in any event, are so insubstantial.

I have deliberately left the Soviet Union out of the discussion until now because its circumstances are so very different. Of the three factors I have discussed, the Soviets possess *only* the market, for whatever that may be worth. It could, in the abstract, be a vast market over the coming years, but I doubt that it will become so in any time frame relevant to this discussion. The Soviets certainly cannot be accused of having a society oriented toward engineering, nor are they well known for their entrepreneurial culture.

Foreign Policy Consequences

It is, therefore, hard to see how the Soviets can ever be a major player in the information revolution. Its computer industry is hardly in the first rank and is not likely under the best of circumstances to become so. Thus, it is probably condemned, no matter how much technology it can steal, to be several generations behind its Western betters at any given moment. But what of it? The Soviets have always lagged far behind the West in most areas of high technology and have nonetheless been able to build and maintain their superpower status.

The past may not, however, be wholly relevant this time. While I do not believe that the Soviet Union is on the verge of sinking into insignificance, I do suggest that the transition into the twenty-first century presents the nation with some extremely difficult problems that probably cannot be solved by old methods.

The information revolution, by its very nature, will have ramifications far beyond the new information systems themselves. The importance of the new technology is that it generates *knowledge*—knowledge that will open up new opportunities for technical advance across a broad spectrum. Industries of all kinds will benefit, and these in turn will generate new advances and new breakthroughs. The consequences will be, in the truest sense of the word, synergistic.

For this to happen one thing will be essential: information will have to flow freely. The new information technology will prove so productive in the United States because the impediments to information flow are minimal. Proprietary rights will, of course, have to be protected, as will national security data, but these limitations will not fundamentally restrict information flow and use.

Can the Soviet system tolerate such a free flow of information? To ask the question is to answer it. Aside from the normal Russian paranoia and historical penchant for secrecy, other more fundamental factors are at work. The most obvious is that in a dictatorship any instrument that facilitates information flow outside the control of the ruling oligarchy strikes, over time, at the very fundamentals of the system. Yet if the information is kept in the hands of the few it loses the creative aspect that graces it with such promise.

Mr. Gorbachev may put a computer at every school desk. He may even succeed, though I doubt it, in training the bureaucracy to use the computer as a management tool. Can he, however, permit computers in homes or individual offices, with open access to data banks and the ability to cross-talk freely? Not unless he is prepared fundamentally to change the nature of the system that promoted him to his current position.

This, then, is the Soviet conundrum: make whatever use you can of new information system technologies, but always under firm state control, thereby forgoing the advantages of a free flow of information, or loosen the control network, free your citizens' inventive capacities, and run the risk that you will not long be in power. I have no doubt which path the Soviet leadership would choose if it even thought in such terms—which it does not.

Under these circumstances I find it hard to conceive of a way out of the box for the Soviets. They will certainly develop a computer capacity substantially better than they now possess and will use it to good effect for military purposes. Nevertheless, the development of a broad new information technology that transforms the nature of the society is, I believe, almost certainly beyond their capacities. Thus, as we close out the twentieth century and enter the twenty-first, we are likely to see increasingly clear evidence of the fundamental inefficiency of totalitarianism. The Soviet Union will come ever more to resemble the dinosaur, incapable of adjusting to the surrounding environment.

This is not an unalloyed message of hope. The dinosaurs died slowly, and were dangerous in the interim. The Soviet military machine will, for many years to come, remain the awesome instrument it now is (though I would add, parenthetically, that even here I believe the information revolution will, over time, provide those who know how to use it with great advances in weapons technology). Given the strains I believe we will see with allies and the developing world in the years ahead—in part caused by the information revolution—the Soviets will have fertile ground for mischief making at our expense. In other words, the Soviet Union will remain our principal foreign threat for decades to come, and as its relative position vis-à-vis the United States diminishes, it may well become more rather than less dangerous.

What that will mean for the United States is what it has always meant—a steady commitment to the maintenance of a defense establishment that even the most frustrated Soviet leadership would fear to challenge. It should mean, as well, that we resolve *not* to make the "transition" for the Soviets more palatable by finding ways to reduce the pressure on them. It should also mean major efforts at rebuilding our transatlantic and Pacific coalitions along new lines more appropriate to the twenty-first century, and substantial attention to finding ways to ensure that the developing world has some hope that it, too, will benefit from the new information age.

The thing I find most disturbing about the analysis I have presented today is the conclusion that Western Europe is falling further behind in the information technology race. This disease is not limited solely to information systems, but infects other high-technology areas as well.

Europe's difficulties should be no cause for rejoicing but rather a source of grave concern. I have for some time believed that the transatlantic relationship, despite the contemporary calm, is in for rough sailing as the century closes. The relationship is strained by generational changes on both sides of the Atlantic, the global nature of America's role versus the regional nature of European interests, increasing differences in how the security threat is perceived and dealt with, and increasing though seldom-stated European disquiet with American unpredictability and naivete. American frustration with Europe's unwillingness to accept its "responsibilities," trade differences of growing asperity, and increasing American interest in the Pacific also bode less than well over the longer term for a constructive transatlantic relationship.

Add to these strains the tensions that would be created by a Western Europe left behind in the information technology race and the resulting brew could be dangerous. An increasingly uncompetitive European partner would be an increasingly uncertain and protectionist Europe that would inevitably be drawn toward a closer relationship—at least economic—with the Soviet bloc. America, at least as much as Europe, would be the loser.

It would behoove us, then, to examine what we can do to encourage Europe to strengthen its high-tech capacities. We cannot, of course, force the EEC to return to the dream of Monnet and get about building Europe again—which would be the single most important step that could be taken. We can, however, *encourage* Europe in that direction and be critical when it falters. We can support and indeed encourage U.S. industry to make cooperative R & D arrangements with European firms, and we can give European industry a fair chance to capture U.S. defense contracts when their bids are competitive. We can resist with all our strength the rising demand in this country and abroad for protectionism, for nothing could more quickly destroy all hope of cooperation in dealing with the challenges of the new era we are entering than for the democracies to engage in economic warfare among themselves.

Our future relationship with Japan is an equally pressing issue, and one that may well get out of hand before we are able to do much about it. It may be, as the Japanese claim, that our trade deficit is no one's fault but our own. Nevertheless, the Japanese give us little opportunity to test the claim; their stubborn refusal to grant meaningful concessions—made worse by constantly conciliatory rhetoric—provides the protectionists with substantial ammunition.

Yet, as we examine the future, particularly in such specific areas as information systems technology, it becomes quickly evident that the United States is in a potentially predominant position that could only be adversely affected by any protectionist steps we might take. We can only hope, therefore, that the Japanese will soon realize how dangerous the game they are playing is and come to grips with reality. If they do not, and if pressures for protectionism become irresistible, then we should take steps explicitly aimed at Japan alone; we should resist at all costs the temptation to fashion measures that have a wider sweep. We should also be ready, as soon as the Japanese make adequate compromises, to return to the *status quo ante*.

The tragedy of the current trade dispute with Japan is that it diverts our attention from the truly important: the future of our relationship with Japan and the countries of the Pacific Basin. I find it hard to believe that our traditional postwar relationship with Japan can last the century. The anachronism of a continuing substantial commitment of American forces to the defense of the North Pacific rim while Japan spends less than 1 percent of its GNP on defense will find ever less enthusiastic adherents here, with growing U.S. pressure for Japan to share more of the military burden. Such messages from Washington now fall on less than receptive ears in Tokyo, but this may change. To expect a nation as economically powerful as Japan to eschew forever a military establishment of some significance may be rational but lacks historical precedent.

These considerations may appear far removed from issues of high technology and the information revolution, but they are not. Our relationships across the Atlantic and the Pacific are going to become increasingly strained over the rest of this century under the best of circumstances; too many things are in flux and transition to believe otherwise. Add the potentially destabilizing revolution in information systems and you have a prognosis that deserves serious high-level concern on both sides of both oceans, beginning now. I am no great lover of international conferences, having sat through too many of them. I nevertheless believe that we and our Pacific and Atlantic friends need—and soon—to fashion some method for collective examination of the challenges of the next several decades, and what steps might be taken, jointly and severally, to make the century we are entering a better and safer one than the century we will soon be leaving behind.

One final word about the foreign policy consequences of the information revolution. The developed world has for too long failed to take seriously the growing gulf between ourselves and the developing world; that disparity can only get worse in the years ahead. The information revolution can increase the rate at which we grow apart, or, if wisely used, help to reduce it. Just as we and our Western European and Japanese allies need to concentrate on our common future, so should we jointly examine how we can begin the common task of reversing a trend that if permitted to continue can only lead to an explosion that will threaten the security of us all.

America is on the edge of a great experience that will change the world in which we live. We will benefit as a nation no matter what we do. Whether we are more secure as a result, or simply an island of growing technological excellence and economic prosperity in a sea of turmoil and poverty, remains to be seen. If we have the imagination and wit to manage wisely the riches that will come to us, then we will have achieved that greatest of accomplishments: to pass on to future generations a world better than the one we inherited.